# The SWORD of Swords

---

The Word of GOD is living and
powerful and sharper than any
two-edged sword..... HEB. 4:12

## Author/Evangelist Thomas Couch

The Spotted Feather, an imprint of Colorful Crow

Publishing

I would like to dedicate this book to the readers. I would also like to dedicate it to my Precious Mother and all of my family. And with all due gratitude I would like to dedicate it to every person that is involved in the ministries worldwide. For their hard work, dedication, and love and kindness to all of those who sought the LORD, and found HIM as a result of the many great ministries out there.

May GOD bless you all beyond measure.

Sincerely In Christ,

Evangelist Thomas Couch

REVIVE - ALL MINISTRIES

ISAIAH 57:15

\* All Scripture is given from the King James Version of the Bible.

**The Word of GOD is living and powerful and sharper than any two-edged sword..... HEB. 4:12**

# Table of Contents

# Introduction

It is my hope, Prayers, and desire that this book will be a blessing to someone.

I pray that it will show the reader how to successfully apply The Word of GOD, The Bible to every area of their lives.

I pray that it will help the reader to overcome weaknesses in whatever area they have, that may hinder them from a closer walk with GOD.

I pray that it will help the reader to become Spiritually aware of Satan's tricks and attempts to harm them or hinder their walk with GOD.

I pray that it will help someone to live the abundant victorious life that Christ gives. I pray that the reader will learn to use the Bible as the Sword of the Spirit and enjoy it's rewards. I hope you enjoy reading The SWORD of swords.

Sincerely,

Evangelist Thomas Couch

REVIVE - ALL MINISTRIES

ISAIAH 57:15

* All Scripture is given from The King James Version of the Bible.

# Chapter One

# The SWORD of Swords

A nd take the helmet of Salvation, and the sword of the Spirit, which is the word of God: EPHESIANS 6:17

My friend this verse refers to the Bible, the Word of GOD, as the Sword of the Spirit. This may be the most important description of the Bible that is used in the Bible. The reason is, when we learn to use the Bible as the Sword, we can have the full rewards of the Bible and experience the abundant victorious life that Jesus Christ wants us to have.

Using the Bible as a sword may just be the most important lesson ever learned. The first thing you need to know about the sword, is that it is perfect and sure. Let's look at a verse to prove this.

The law of the Lord is perfect. Converting the soul: the testimony of the Lord is sure, making wise the simple. PSALMS 19:7

The law of the Lord spoken of in this verse is referring to the whole Bible from cover to cover. This verse says the Bible is perfect. It is perfect for anything you need it for. It has the answer and solution to any question or problem you will ever face in this life. The Bible is perfect.

The second thing this verse uses to refer to the Bible is, the testimony of the Lord. That also is referring to the whole Bible from cover to cover. This verse says the Bible is sure. It is sure to use in any area of your life. It is sure to bring victory to any situation. The Bible is sure.

There are many descriptions that the Bible gives of itself. When you see these descriptions, you can take them all literally as referring to the whole Bible from cover to cover. Here are a few of them listed below:

The Sword of the Spirit.

The Word of GOD.

The Law.

The Commandments.

Precepts.

Statutes.

Words of Wisdom.

Words of Knowledge.

The Gospel.

My friend, there are many more of these descriptions of the Bible. They can all refer to the whole Bible. There are many Commandments in the Bible, not just the Ten Commandments.

Jesus said that man shall not live by bread alone, but by every word that proceeds from the mouth of God. Let's look at that verse.

But He answered and said, It is written, man shall not live by bread alone, but by every word that proceeds from the mouth of God. MATTHEW 4:4

Every word of the Bible is important. Every word of it came from GOD. Jesus said everything that HE said came from the Father. HE just listened to the Father and spoke what GOD gave HIM to speak.

That is what we are supposed to live by. Let's look at that verse that I am referring to:

Believest thou not that I am in the Father, and the Father in Me? The words that I speak unto you I speak not of myself: but the Father that dwelleth in me, he doeth the works. JOHN 14:10

What Jesus is saying is, the words that HE speaks, HE does not speak on HIS own authority, but the Father gives them to HIM.

The whole Bible from cover to cover is inspired by GOD Himself. Some people refer to it as being GOD breathed. Let's look at that verse.

All Scripture is given by inspiration of God, and is profitable for doctrine, for reproof, for correction, for instruction in righteousness: 2nd TIMOTHY 3:16

The Bible from cover to cover is given by GOD. It is for us to live by.

This verse gives a few things the Bible is profitable for, when we use it in our lives. It is profitable for doctrine, for reproof, for correction, and for instruction in righteousness. The Bible is perfect and sure in all of these things that it gives for us to live by.

Jesus said the words that HE speaks to us are Spirit. That is how they make things happen in our lives. When they are used as the sword, they make things happen. Let's look at that verse:

It is the Spirit that quickeneth; the flesh profiteth nothing: the words that I speak unto you, they are Spirit, and they are life. JOHN 6:63

The whole Bible from cover to cover is Spirit. That is why it is called the Sword of the Spirit. When it is used as the sword, things take place in the Spirit realm and come to pass in the natural realm. The Word of GOD has unlimited power to make things happen in our lives. It is powerful.

The Bible is the most powerful thing on this earth when it is used as the Sword. It moves GOD to work things out in our lives. Let's look at a verse to see the Power of the Sword.

For the word of God is quick, and powerful, and sharper than any two-edged sword, piercing even to the dividing asunder of soul and Spirit, and of the joints and marrow, and is a discerner of the thoughts and intents of the heart. HEBREWS 4:12

My friend, the sword is indeed the most powerful thing on this earth. It is very important for Christians to learn how to use the Sword. In order to learn how to use the Sword, we must study it.

Let's look at a verse to prove this:

Study to shew thyself approved unto God, a workman that needeth not to be ashamed, rightly dividing the word of truth. 2nd TIMO-THY 2:15

We have to study the Word of GOD daily to learn how to use it as the Sword. This verse says we must learn how to rightly divide the Word of Truth. That is the Bible from cover to cover. You see, there is rightly dividing it, and wrongly dividing it. Satan will always come at you and wrongly divide the word to get you to sin. That is why we must study it, and learn to rightly divide it, so we can use it as a sword. That is why GOD gave it, to use as a sword. So we can overcome Satan and his unclean army, and live the abundant victorious life that Jesus Christ wants us to live.

Satan is out to get all Christians. The Bible says he came to steal, kill, and to destroy. But in that same verse, Jesus said that HE Himself came that we might have abundant life. Let's look at that verse.

The thief cometh not, but to steal, and to kill, and to destroy: I am come that they might have life, and that they might have it more abundantly. JOHN 10:10

My friend, Satan wants to destroy your life. He is out to do anything in his power to make you suffer in every area of your life. Satan will always wrongly divide The Word to destroy you in every area of your life, and try to pull you away from GOD. That is why it is so important to learn to use the Sword.

Praise GOD! My friend, Jesus said that HE came to give us abundant life. If you want that abundant life, you must learn to use the Sword. If not, Satan will take it from you.

It is a must to learn everything you can about using the Sword. It will, without a doubt, bring victory to any situation you face in life. So if you want that abundant victorious life, you must learn to use the Sword. Then you will enjoy all the promises in GOD'S Word, and you will enjoy its full rewards. Because it is indeed The SWORD of swords.

Hallelujah!

# Chapter Two

---

# How to Use the Sword

1.) Then was Jesus led up of the Spirit into the wilderness to be tempted of the devil.

2.) And when he had fasted forty days and forty nights, he was afterward an hungred.

3.) And when the tempter came to him, he said, If thou be the Son of God, command that these stones be made bread.

4.) But he answered and said, It is written, Man shall not live by bread alone, but by every word that proceedeth out of the mouth of God.

5.) Then the devil taketh him up into the holy city, and setteth him on a Pinnacle of the temple,

6.) And saith unto him, If thou be the Son of God, cast thyself down: for it is written, He shall give his angels charge concerning thee: and in their hands they shall bear thee up, lest at any time thou dash thy foot against a stone.

7.) Jesus said unto him, It is written again, Thou shalt not tempt the Lord thy God.

8.) Again, the devil taketh him up into an exceeding high mountain, and sheweth him all the kingdoms of the world, and the glory of them;

9.) And saith unto him, All these things will I give thee, if thou wilt fall down and worship me.

10.) Then saith Jesus unto him, Get thee hence, Satan: for it is written, Thou shalt worship the Lord thy God, and him only shalt thou serve.

11.) Then the devil leaveth him, and, behold, angels came and ministered unto him.

MATTHEW 4:1-11

My dear Christian friend, this is the best example in the Bible of how to use the sword. Jesus Himself uses it when Satan came to tempt Him.

Notice how Satan wrongly divided the Word of GOD and tried to get Jesus to wrongly apply it.

Satan will always try to get you to wrongly apply GOD'S Word. Satan knows the Word of GOD, but he cannot successfully use it against us, if we know for ourselves how to use it, and rightly apply it to our lives.

Jesus Himself shows us how to use the Sword of the Spirit in these verses. We are to speak it. We are to speak it to Satan and his unclean army anytime he comes against us. We are to speak it to situations that come up in our lives.

When we speak the Word of GOD and use it as the Sword of the Spirit, it moves GOD on our behalf. When we use the Sword of the Spirit properly, it makes things happen in the Spiritual realm, and then they manifest in the natural realm.

My dear Christian friend, it is essential that we learn to use the Word of GOD as the Sword of the Spirit in our lives. Because Satan and his unclean army are going to come against us as long as we are on this earth. Satan is going to try to steal, kill and destroy our lives in any way he can. Satan and his unclean army are going to confront us, and you can count on that.

I will give you an example of how to use the Sword of the Spirit when Satan comes against you to get you to sin. This is a good verse to use, let's look at it.

Submit yourselves therefore to God. Resist the devil, and he will flee from you. JAMES 4:7

If Satan has come against you to tempt you to sin, the confrontation should go something like this. Quote this verse.

"Satan, the word of God says that if I submit to God and resist you then you will have to flee from me. So I submit to God and I resist you Satan, and I command you to flee. In Jesus' name."

My dear Christian friend, that is how we are to properly use the Sword of the Spirit in our lives. We are to speak it to Satan and his unclean army and to situations that come up in our lives.

Do not be ashamed to speak the Word of GOD out loud. That is exactly what Satan wants. He wants us to be ashamed to speak the Word of GOD out loud, so that we cannot successfully use it as the Sword of the Spirit, and overcome him and his unclean army. He wants us to be ashamed to speak the Word of GOD out loud so that he can steal, kill, and destroy us in every area of our lives.

The Sword of the Spirit is indeed the most powerful thing on this earth when we successfully use it in our lives. We are to apply it to every area of our lives so we can live and enjoy that abundant victorious life that Jesus wants us to have.

One thing you must always remember is, to ask GOD to forgive you for your sins before you use the Sword of the Spirit. If you have unforgiven sin in your life, the Sword will not work until you have asked GOD to forgive you for that sin. It is a good thing to ask GOD to forgive you for all your sins before you pray or use the Sword or anything. You see, sin separates us from GOD. If you have unforgiven sin in your life, you are not in Christ. When you sin, you step out of Christ and you are no longer under the blood. But, when you ask for forgiveness for your sins, you are back in Christ, and are safely under the blood. Then you can use the Sword of the Spirit successfully in your life again.

A good example of this would be between David and Goliath. See, Goliath tried to use the Sword on David first, by quoting Scripture. But Goliath did not have a Covenant with GOD, so he could not successfully use the Sword on David.

David did have a Covenant with GOD. So he reversed the situation and used the Sword on Goliath. Let's look at that passage and see what it says.

44.) And the Philistine said to David, come to me, and I will give thy flesh unto the fowls of the air, and to the beasts of the field.

45.) Then said David to the Philistine, Thou comest to me with a sword, and with a spear, and with a shield: but I come to thee in the name of the Lord of hosts, the God of the armies of Israel, whom thou hast defied.

46.) This day will the Lord deliver thee into mine hand; and I will smite thee, and take thine head from thee; and I will give the carcasses of the host of the Philistines this day unto the fowls of the air, and to the wild beasts of the earth; that all the earth may know that there is a God in Israel.

1st SAMUEL 17:44-46

You see, before the actual fight began, the Sword was used by both David and Goliath. They quoted Scripture to one another. Just like Satan quoted Scripture to Jesus in our opening verses. Let's look at the verse they quoted from.

And thy carcase shall be meat unto all fowls of the air, and unto the beasts of the earth, and no man shall fray them away. DEUTERONOMY 28:26

So you see, Goliath could not use the Sword successfully. But David could. Goliath was coming against a man of GOD. But Goliath did not have a Covenant with GOD. David did have a Covenant with GOD, and David told him that he came to fight in the name of the Lord.

So you see, if you have unforgiven sin in your life, and you have stepped out of Christ, which is what you do when you sin, then you will not be able to successfully use the Sword.

I can tell you this from experience. Do not be surprised at who Satan will use to come against you with Scripture. He may use a Christian friend, or a family member or anybody. But the thing to do is, you must always recognize the Spirit that is working against you. So do not rebuke the person, but the Spirit. That is what Jesus did when Peter tried to rebuke HIM. Jesus recognized that it was Satan working through Peter trying to rebuke HIM. So Jesus rebuked Satan, not Peter. Let's look at those verses.

22.) Then Peter took him, and began to rebuke him, saying, Be it far from thee, Lord: this shall not be unto thee.

23.) But he turned, and said unto Peter, Get thee behind me, Satan: thou art an offence unto me: for thou savourest not the things that be of God, but those that be of men. MATTHEW 17:22-23

So you see Jesus spoke directly to the Spirit that was coming against HIM. Peter was saying it, but it was Satan working through him to get to Jesus.

I can assure you my dear Christian friend, if you live long enough, you will experience this. Do not be surprised at who Satan may use to come against you. Like I said, it may be a Christian friend, or a family member or anybody. Just be sure that you know the Word of GOD for yourself, and rebuke the Spirit that is coming against you and not the person.

If you are a Christian, it is a must that you know how to use the Sword. You must study it. Then you must break it down and rightly divide it. Then you must rightly apply it. You must learn to quote the Scriptures to any situation you encounter, and to Satan, and his unclean army.

You must learn to speak the Word of GOD my friend, and successfully use it as the Sword. Then you will be able to live that abundant victorious life that Jesus wants you to live. And you will enjoy all the Bible's full rewards, because it is indeed The Sword of swords.

Glory to GOD!

# Chapter Three

---

# Speaking to Sickness

1.) Bless the Lord, O my Soul: and all that is within me, bless his holy name.

2.) Bless the Lord, O my Soul, and forget not all his benefits:

3.) Who forgiveth all thine iniquities; Who healeth all thy diseases.
PSALMS 103:1-3

My friend, according to the third verse in this passage, the Lord is the one who heals all of our diseases. I do not think GOD wants anybody to be sick. But unfortunately, we do sometimes get sick. I do not think it is GOD'S will, but it sometimes happens to us.

Most of the time when we get sick, our first reaction is to pray for our healing. That is exactly what we are supposed to do is pray. But we are also supposed to use the Sword for our healing as well.

When we pray for healing, we are supposed to remind GOD of HIS word. We are supposed to remind GOD that HIS word says HE is the one who heals all of our diseases. We are also supposed to speak to our sickness. We are supposed to get in the Word of GOD and look up all the verses concerning GOD'S healing power and then quote them to our sickness. That is how we use the Sword on our sickness.

Our words should be words of healing. They should go something like this.

Sickness, I speak to you in Jesus' name. The Word of GOD says that the Lord heals all of my diseases. So sickness, I command you to leave my body and I speak healing into my being. In Jesus' name.

That, my friend, is how to use the Sword on our sickness. We are to quote healing verses from GOD'S Word.

Sometimes our healing involves our obedience to GOD'S Word. If it involves obedience to GOD'S Word, then we may have been disobedient to GOD'S Word in some area of our lives and that may be how the sickness came upon us. If we are disobedient to GOD'S Word, then we have sinned, and when we sin, we step out of Christ and open ourselves up for sickness to come in.

Let's look at the verse that says our healing may involve obedience to GOD'S Word.

And said, If thou wilt diligently hearken to the voice of the Lord thy God, and wilt do that which is right in his sight, and wilt give ear to his commandments, and keep all his statutes, I will put none of these diseases upon thee, which I have brought upon the Egyptians: for I am the Lord that healeth thee. EXODUS 15:26

GOD promises to heal HIS people from sickness. HE does not want anybody to be sick. Our healing may depend on our obedience to GOD'S Word. We have to believe that GOD wants to heal us to start with. Then we are to look up healing Scriptures and quote them to our sickness. We are to speak GOD'S Word to our sickness. We are not supposed to speak words of doubt and keep saying we are sick.

My friend, the Bible says that death and life are in the power of the tongue. So when we are sick, we are to speak words of life and not words of death. Let's look at a verse to prove this.

Death and life are in the power of the tongue: and they that love it shall eat the fruit thereof. PROVERBS 18:21

So you see, the words that we speak do have power. So when we are sick, GOD wants us to speak HIS word, words of healing and not sickness and doubt.

The Bible says that the Spirit of a man will sustain his infirmity. So we are to be of a good Spirit and speak words of life to our sickness. Let's look at that verse.

The Spirit of a man will sustain his infirmity; but a wounded Spirit who can bear? PROVERBS 18:14

So you see, the way that we look at sickness and speak about it has an effect on our healing.

Like I said, GOD does not want us to be sick. But we do sometimes get sick. So when we do, we are to use the Sword and speak the Word of GOD to our sickness. We are to speak healing verses, which are words of life. We are not to speak words of death. We are not supposed to agree that we are sick. We are supposed to agree that GOD is healing us.

Jesus Himself took our sickness so that we could be healed when we do get sick. The Bible says that with HIS stripes we are healed. Jesus took the stripes for us before he was killed. Jesus took those stripes because HE wanted us to be healed and not sick. GOD does not want anybody to be sick. That is why Jesus took those stripes. HE took our sickness so that we could be healed and walk in good health. Let's look at a verse to prove this.

But he was wounded for our transgressions, he was bruised for our iniquities: the Chastisement of our Peace was upon him; and with his stripes we are healed. ISAIAH 53:5

So you see, Jesus took on our sickness. HE took it on so that we could be healed. This verse does not say that we might be healed. It says that by HIS stripes we are healed. Remember, GOD does not want us to be sick. That is why Jesus took on our sickness. HE took it on so that we could be healed when we do get sick. It is up to us to use the Sword and speak words of life and not words of death. We are to quote healing verses to our sickness. We are supposed to agree that by HIS stripes we are healed. I can assure you that you will not find any verses in the Bible that says GOD wants us to be sick. But we will find verse on top of verse that says GOD wants us healed. The Word of GOD is health to our bodies. The Word of GOD does not bring sickness, it brings good health. Let's look at some verses to prove this.

20.) My Son, attend to my words; incline thine ear unto my sayings.

21.) Let them not depart from thine eyes; Keep them in the midst of thine heart.

22.) For they are life unto those that find them, and health to all their flesh.

PROVERBS 4:20-22

So you see, the Word of GOD is health to our flesh. That is why we are to use the Sword on our sickness. The Sword brings good health to our flesh. The Word of GOD is life, and that is what we are supposed to speak when we are sick. The words of GOD is the Sword and that is how we are to use the Sword on our sickness. We are to quote healing verses to our sickness. That is how our healing comes about. It is when we use the Sword and speak to our sickness.

My dear Christian friend, the Word of GOD speaks for itself. GOD never wants us to be sick. Instead, when we do get sick, GOD wants us to know how to use the Sword on our sickness. When we learn to use the Sword on our sickness, then we will overcome it and live that abundant victorious life that Jesus wants us to have, and we will have all the Bible's full rewards. Because it is indeed The Sword of swords.

Praise GOD!

# Chapter Four

---

# Speaking to Finances

L et them shout for joy, and be glad, that favour my righteous cause: yea, let them say continually, Let the Lord be magnified, which hath pleasure in the prosperity of his servant. PSALMS 35:27

My dear Christian friend, I do not think GOD wants anybody to be poor. According to this verse, GOD has pleasure in the prosperity of HIS servants. GOD wants us to prosper in every area of our lives. Jesus said that HE came so we might have abundant life and that includes our finances.

I can tell you this, GOD always wants to prosper HIS people. Job was a man of GOD, and the Bible says that he was the greatest of all the men of the East. Let's look at that verse.

His substance also was seven thousand sheep, and three thousand camels, and five hundred yoke of oxen, and five hundred she asses, and a very great household, so that this man was the greatest of all the men of the east. JOB 1:3

So you see, Job was a man of GOD. GOD had prospered Job in every area of his life. And GOD wants to do the same thing for us. Satan is the one who will try to have us thinking that GOD wants us to be poor.

Satan wants us to think that GOD wants us to be poor because that is contrary to what GOD'S Word says about our finances. You see, the truth is, that GOD'S Word promises that we will have wealth and riches. Let's look at some verses to prove this.

1.) Praise ye the Lord. Blessed is the man that feareth the Lord, that delighteth greatly in his commandments.

2.) His seed shall be mighty upon earth: the generation of the upright shall be blessed.

3.) Wealth and riches shall be in his house: and his righteousness endureth for ever.

PSALMS 112:1-3

Praise GOD my friend! That is good news. These verses says that wealth and riches shall be in our houses. That is a promise. I will not go as far as to say that everybody will be filthy rich. You see, GOD knows our hearts. GOD does not want us to trust in our riches. HE wants us to trust in HIM for everything.

You see, if we trust in our riches instead of trusting in GOD, we will fall. That is what the Word of GOD says and it is the truth. Let's look at that verse.

He that trusteth in his riches shall fall: but the righteous shall flourish as a branch. PROVERBS 11:28

My friend, the truth is, that if we trust in our riches instead of GOD, we will fall. I do not think that GOD would give us anything that would make us fall. So if we are not prospering like we think we should, it may be that GOD is withholding it until we grow enough that we won't put our trust in our riches. GOD wants to give us good gifts and

GOD wants us to prosper in every area of our lives. But GOD is not going to give us anything that would make us fall away from HIM. GOD does want to give us good gifts. The Word of GOD says that every good gift comes from GOD. Let's look at that verse.

Every good gift and every perfect gift is from above, and cometh down from the Father of lights, with whom is no variableness, neither shadow of turning. JAMES 1:17

So you see, according to this verse, every good and perfect gift is from GOD. GOD desires to give us good and perfect gifts. But if it is something that would make us fall, it would not be a good and perfect gift. That may just be why GOD is not blessing us in our finances right now. However, when we get to the place where GOD knows we will put all of our trust in HIM and not in our riches, then GOD can start prospering us in our finances. It will happen because GOD'S Word says that wealth and riches will be in our houses, and that is a promise from GOD Himself. My friend, there is another verse that says that there will be rich people in this world. It also says that GOD gives to us richly to enjoy all things. And also in that same verse, it commands us not to trust in our riches, but to trust in GOD. Let's look at that verse.

Charge them that are rich in this world, that they be not high minded, nor trust in uncertain riches, but in the living God, who giveth us richly all things to enjoy; 1st TIMOTHY 6:17

So you see, according to this verse, there will be rich people in this world. It says that GOD gives us richly all things to enjoy. But this is also a Commandment in this verse, for us not to trust in our riches, but to trust in GOD. The Commandment is there, because GOD knows that if we trust in our riches instead of trusting in HIM, we will fall. We will fall away from GOD if we trust in our riches. I know we do not want to fall away from GOD. My friend there is a verse that says, it is a fearful thing to fall into the hands of the living God. (HEBREWS 10:31) But I can tell you it is even a more fearful thing to fall out of the hands of the living GOD. So we know that trusting in our riches will make us fall. We also know that GOD may be withholding our finances until HE knows we won't trust in our finances.

There is one thing we can rejoice about no matter what comes our way. That is that GOD knows our need before we even ask HIM and GOD will meet all of our needs. Let's look at a verse to prove this.

Be not ye therefore like unto them: for your Father knoweth what things ye have need of, before ye ask him. MATTHEW 6:8

Praise GOD! My friend, according to this verse, GOD knows what things we have need of before we even ask for them. That is good news. But, it is even better news to know that GOD promises to meet every one of our needs. Let's look at a verse to prove that GOD will meet our every need.

But my God shall supply all your need according to his riches in glory by Christ Jesus. PHILIPPIANS 4:19

Praise GOD! Christian people, this verse is a promise that GOD will supply all of our needs. That is one thing we can count on, even if we are not being blessed in our finances right now.

There is also another issue that we need to look at. That is that Satan will try to take away our finances. In the book of JOB, Chapter one, the first thing that Satan did when he came against Job was, he attacked his finances. Satan took away his animals. Those animals were worth a lot of money, and Satan thought that by taking them, that he could make Job fall away from GOD.

But Job did not trust in his riches, he trusted in GOD, so that is why he did not fall away from GOD. That is the lesson that we must learn from Job. That we do not trust in our riches, but we trust in GOD.

Another lesson that we can learn from Job is that Satan will come against us and try to take away our finances. That is when we are supposed to use the Sword of the Spirit and speak to Satan and tell him to take his hands off of our finances. Then we are to use the Sword and speak directly to our needed finances and command them to come to us.

The confrontation should go something like this.

"Satan, the Word of GOD shows that you will come against my finances. The Word of GOD also says that I will have wealth and riches in my house. So Satan, I speak to you and I command you to take your hands off of my finances, In Jesus' name."

Then we are to use the Sword and speak directly to our needed finances and command them to come to us. And that should go something like this.

"Needed finances, I speak to you. The Word of GOD says that I will have wealth and riches in my house, and the Word of GOD also says that my GOD will supply my every need. So I speak to you needed finances and I command you to Come to me, In Jesus' name."

That, my friend, is how we are to confront Satan when he comes against our finances. And that is how we are to use the Sword and speak to our finances.

My dear friend, this may seem somewhat foolish to you if you do not understand the Christian's authority to use the Word of GOD as the Sword of the Spirit.

If it seems foolish to you to use the Sword and speak to your finances, I remind you that Jesus Himself spoke to fig trees, (MATTHEW 21:17-20; MARK 11:13-14, 20-23), and glory to GOD the fig tree did exactly what Jesus told it to do.

My dear Christian friend, you and I have the authority to send forth GOD'S Word with our mouth and according to the Word, it will accomplish what we please, and prosper in the things we send it to. Let's look at that passage.

10.) For as the rain cometh down, and the snow from heaven, and returneth not thither, but watereth the earth, and maketh it bring forth and bud, that it may give seed to the sower, and bread to the eater:

11.) So shall my word be that goeth forth out of my mouth: it shall not return unto me void, but it shall accomplish that which I please, and it shall prosper in the thing whereto I sent it.

ISAIAH 55:10-11

So, as we see, according to this passage, GOD sends HIS word, "out of HIS mouth," and it returns, but not void. It accomplishes what HE pleases, and prospers in the things HE sends it to.

So we as GOD'S people, have the same power to send forth GOD'S Word to whatever pleases us, and things to prosper us, and it will accomplish what we please, and prosper in the things we send it to, and Hallelujah it will not return void.

So you see, it doesn't seem so foolish when we are told that GOD Himself sends HIS Word out of HIS mouth.

GOD also commanded ravens to take the Prophet Elijah food that he needed, and those birds took Elijah bread and meat twice a day.

(1st KINGS 17:2-6)

So those birds obeyed GOD'S Word. They will obey ours also. Some people are skilled in training birds to do what they say.

There is another passage that shines some light on how GOD can get us things that we need.

We may be looking for GOD to meet our needs in average every day ways, but, HE may send our finances or whatever we need in ways that we never dreamed of.

Jesus told Peter to go catch a fish and look in it's mouth and he would find the money they needed to pay their taxes. (MATTHEW 17:24-27) So I am quite sure GOD Himself commanded the fish to take Peter the money, just as HE commanded the ravens to take Elijah the things he needed.

Jesus tells us in another verse that we can speak to mountains and tell them to move from one place to another and that they will move. Let's look at that verse.

And Jesus said unto them, Because of your unbelief: for verily I say unto you, If ye have faith as a grain of mustard seed, ye shall say unto this mountain, Remove hence to yonder place; and it shall remove; and nothing shall be impossible unto you. MATTHEW 17:20

So according to this verse, we can tell mountains, (things) to move from one place to another. Thus, we can command a mountain of debt to be moved out of our lives. Then we can tell the needed finances to be moved into our lives, and Glory to GOD, this verse goes on to say that nothing shall be impossible for us.

Praise the Lord! Dear friend, this is good news.

Let me tell you not to be surprised at how GOD may get those finances to you once you speak to them. It is up to us to use the Sword and speak to our finances, but it is up to GOD to get them to us.

Always remember that HIS ways are higher than our ways and HIS thoughts than our thoughts. (ISAIAH 55:8-9)

Keep in mind also, that HE is able to do exceeding abundantly above all that we ask or think. (EPHESIANS 3:20)

The Sword is the most powerful thing on this earth. We must learn to use it in every area of our lives, including our finances. Then we can live that abundant victorious life that Jesus wants us to live, and we can enjoy all the Bible's full rewards.

Because it is indeed The Sword of swords.

Hallelujah!

# Chapter Five

---

# Speaking to Yourself

And David was greatly distressed; for the people spake of stoning him, because the soul of all the people was grieved, every man for his sons and for his daughters: but David encouraged himself in the Lord his God. 1st SAMUEL 30:6

My Dear Christian friend, according to this verse, David encouraged himself in the Lord. When everybody else was grieved and down, even speaking of stoning David. Even in the face of death, David found a way to encourage himself in the Lord.

My friend, this is a lesson we all can learn to do. No matter what storms life may bring our way, we can learn to encourage ourselves in the Lord.

The very best way to encourage ourselves in the Lord, is to get in the Word of GOD. You need to study it, think on it, look up the Promises in GOD'S Word, and get it all down in you. That is how we as Christians are to encourage ourselves in the Lord. Speak to yourself.

Read the Bible out loud and ask GOD to write it on the tablet of your heart as you are reading it out loud. GOD tells us in HIS Word, to write HIS Word on the table of our heart. Let's look at that verse.

1.) My son forget not my law; but let thine heart keep my commandments:

2.) For length of days, and long life and peace, shall they add to thee.

3.) Let not mercy and truth forsake thee: bind them about thy neck; write them upon the table of thine heart:

PROVERBS 3:1-3

So we are to write the Word of GOD on the table of our hearts. This is a Command, and we find it again in the Book of PROVERBS in another verse. Let's look at that passage also.

1.) My son, keep my words, and lay up my Commandments with thee.

2.) Keep my Commandments, and live; and my law as the apple of thine eye.

3.) Bind them upon thy fingers, write them upon the table of thine heart.

PROVERBS 7:1-3

So again, we see the command to write the Word of GOD on the table of our hearts. This is very important to do. GOD knows if we write HIS Word on the table of our hearts, then we can learn to use it as the Sword of the Spirit in times of need.

So, now that we know that we are to write the Word of GOD on the table of our hearts, the question is, how do we write it on our hearts. GOD also tells us how to do this. We are to read it out loud and ask GOD to write it on the table of our heart. Let's look a verse to prove this.

My heart is inditing a good matter: I speak of the things which I have made touching the King: my tongue is the pen of a ready writer.

PSALMS 45:1

My dear friend, according to this verse, our tongue is the pen that we are to use to write the Word of GOD on the table of our hearts. It says my tongue is the pen of a ready writer.

When GOD showed me this verse, I read the entire Bible out loud and I asked GOD to write it on the table of my heart. I put my pen to work. And I encourage you to do the same thing. Jesus said that man shall not live by bread alone, but by every word that proceedeth out of the mouth of God. Let's look at that verse.

But he answered and said, It is written, Man shall not live by bread alone, but by every word that proceedeth out of the mouth of God.

MATTHEW 4:4

Every word that proceedeth out of the mouth of GOD is HIS word. It is the entire Bible from cover to cover. And Jesus said that we are to live by it.

We are to write it on the table of our hearts. And our tongue is the pen. We are to read it out loud and ask GOD to write it on the table of our hearts. As we have seen it is a command for us to write the Word of GOD on the table of our hearts. It is a command for our own good. Because we are to live by it. And we are to use it as the Sword of the Spirit for our victory in Christ.

It also builds your faith when you read the Word of GOD out loud. So I encourage you to read the Word of GOD out loud and build up your faith. Let's look at the verse that says faith comes by hearing the Word of GOD read out loud.

So then faith cometh by hearing, and hearing by the word of God.

ROMANS 10:17

It says faith comes by hearing. The Word of GOD is what we need to hear to build up our faith. We need to read the Word of GOD out loud, to write it on the table of our hearts, and we need to read the

Word of GOD out loud to build up our faith, and we need to read the Word of GOD out loud to encourage ourselves in the Lord like David did. Glory to GOD!

We are to read the Word of GOD out loud, and we are to think on it. We are to think on it to get it in our hearts also. Let's look at a verse to prove this.

Finally, brethren, whatsoever things are true, whatsoever things are honest, whatsoever things are just, whatsoever things are pure, whatsoever things are lovely, whatsoever things are of good report; if there be any virtue, and if there be any Praise, think on these things.

PHILIPPIANS 4:8

My dear friend, the Bible is true, the Bible is honest, the Bible is just, the Bible is pure, the Bible is lovely, the Bible is a good report and we are to think on it. We are to read the Bible out loud and think on it. When we read it out loud, we write it on the table of our hearts and we build our faith up and we also encourage ourselves in the Lord like David did.

Our tongue is the pen that we use to write the Word of GOD on our hearts, because the tongue has Power. There is a verse that says the tongue has Power. Let's look at that verse to prove this.

Death and life are in the Power of the tongue: and they that love it shall eat the fruit thereof. PROVERBS 18:21

So you see, this verse says that death and life are in the Power of the tongue. The tongue has Power. It has the Power to write the Word of GOD on the table of our hearts, it has the Power to build up our faith, and it has the Power to encourage us in the Lord like David did.

The tongue has the Power of life in it. The Word of GOD is life and that is what we are to speak with our tongues. Let's look at a verse that says the Word of GOD is life.

It is the Spirit that quickeneth; the flesh profiteth nothing: the words that I speak unto you, they are Spirit, and they are life. JOHN 6:63

Jesus said that HIS words are life. HIS words make up the entire Word of GOD. So our tongue has Power when we speak the Word of GOD out loud.

The Word of GOD is the life that we are to speak into our situations to have victory in that situation. We are not to speak words of death. Words of death are anything that is contrary to the Word of GOD. The Word of GOD is life and that is what we are to speak into any situation that comes our way.

The verse that we looked at earlier says that death and life are in the Power of the tongue. Death is anything contrary to the Word of GOD. And life is the Word of GOD. So the Word of GOD has Power when we speak it out loud with our tongue.

That is how we overcome Satan, when we use the Word of GOD as the Sword of the Spirit and speak it out loud. That is when it becomes the Sword, is when we use the Power of the tongue and speak it out loud.

So when you speak to yourself, speak the Word of GOD and encourage yourself in the Lord. When you speak the Word of GOD out loud, you are using it as the Sword. When you learn to speak it out loud and use it as the Sword, you can live that abundant victorious life that Jesus wants you to live, and you can enjoy the Bible's full rewards. Because it is indeed The Sword of swords.

Glory to GOD!

# Chapter Six

---

# Speaking to Mountains and Storms

J esus answered and said unto them, verily I say unto you, If ye have
faith, and doubt not, ye shall not only do this which is done to the
fig tree, but also if ye shall say unto this mountain, Be thou removed,
and be thou cast into the sea; it shall be done. MATTHEW 21:21

My dear Christian friend, you can believe Satan is going to put some
mountains in your life.

But the good thing is, you have the Sword of the Spirit to use to
move those mountains out of your life.

According to this verse, if you have faith, that is faith in GOD and
the Power of the Sword. And you do not doubt GOD'S Word, then
you can speak to mountains that come up in your life and command
them to be moved.

One of the mountains that Satan will bring into our lives to steal our peace, is tribulation. But we know that, in Christ we are supposed to have peace, not tribulation. Let's look at a verse to prove this.

These things I have spoken unto you, that in me ye might have peace. In the world ye shall have tribulation: but be of good cheer; I have overcome the world. JOHN 16:33

So you see, Jesus said, In HIM you will have peace. But HE also said that in the world you shall have tribulation. If you are in the world, that means that you have stepped out of Christ. When you step out of Christ, you open yourself up for Satan to bring tribulation against you to steal your peace.

When the tribulation comes, the thing to do is to repent and get back in Christ as soon as you can. Then you use the Sword and speak to that mountain of tribulation and command it to be moved out of your lives in Jesus' name.

The confrontation should go something like this when you are speaking to a mountain of tribulation.

"You mountain of tribulation, I speak to you and I command you to be moved out of my life. And Satan, I speak to you and I command you to take your hands off of my peace, In Jesus' name."

My dear Christian friend, when you do this, you have just used the Word of GOD as the Sword of the Spirit. And when you do, the tribulation has to go and Satan has to bow the knee and take his hands off of your peace.

If you are experiencing tribulation in your life, something is wrong. Because Jesus Himself said that "In HIM" you would have peace. So if the tribulation comes, then you must have stepped out of Christ. Then the best thing to do is get back in Christ and use the Sword of the Spirit to speak to that mountain of tribulation and Satan, so you can overcome the situation.

So in Christ you are supposed to have peace. You are not supposed to have tribulation in Christ. Let's look at another verse to prove this.

And the peace of God, which passeth all understanding, shall keep your hearts and minds through Christ Jesus. PHILIPPIANS 4:7

So you see, it is a fact that you are supposed to have peace in Christ. It is GOD'S Will for us to have peace. It is not GOD'S Will for us to have tribulation. So when that tribulation comes, use the Sword of the Spirit and speak to that mountain and command it to be moved out of your life.

Peace is fruit of the Spirit. So if you are in Christ, and filled with the Holy Spirit, then you should have peace in your life. Satan is the one who will try to take your peace. But that is when you need to know how to use the Sword of the Spirit and take your peace back. When Satan tries to take your peace, you should be bold and strong and tell him what the Word of GOD says about you having peace in your life. That is how you use the Sword of the Spirit. Let's look at another verse to prove that peace is Fruit of the Spirit, and you are supposed to have peace in your life.

22.) But the fruit of the Spirit is love, joy, peace, longsuffering, gentleness, goodness, faith,

23.) Meekness, temperance: against such there is no law.

GALATIANS 5:22-23

So you see, peace is included in with the Fruit of the Spirit. So if you are in Christ and filled with the Spirit, you should have peace in your life, along with all the other stuff named as Fruit of the Spirit in these verses. So if Satan tries to take your Peace, love, joy, faith or any of the Fruit of the Spirit, you can use the Sword of the Spirit and tell Satan that it is written, your peace, love, joy, faith, etc., is Fruit of the Spirit and you will not accept him taking it out of your life. Satan has to bow the knee when you use the Sword of the Spirit against him. The Sword of the Spirit is indeed the most Powerful thing on this earth.

You can also speak to storms. You can speak to literal storms, and you can speak to storms of situations like the mountains we have discussed in this Chapter. Just like Satan will bring mountains in your life, he will also bring storms to pull you away from GOD, or destroy you. Satan can create a literal storm of rain and wind and such. But the good thing is, you can use the Sword of the Spirit and speak to a literal storm and tell it to stop. Let's look at an example that Jesus gave us, showing us how to speak to a literal storm.

23.) And when he was entered into a ship, his disciples followed him.

24.) And, behold, there arose a great tempest in the sea, insomuch that the ship was covered with the waves: but he was asleep.

25.) And his disciples came to him, and awoke him, saying, Lord save us: we perish.

26.) And he saith unto them, why are ye fearful, O ye of little faith? Then he arose, and rebuked the winds and the sea; and there was a great calm.

MATTHEW 8:23-26

So you see, Jesus Himself gave us an example of how to speak to a literal storm. Jesus rebuked the storm, and it went away. So you and I can do the same thing. All we have to do is use the Sword of the Spirit and speak what the Word of GOD says about that Storm. GOD Himself will calm the storm when we speak to it and use the Sword of the Spirit against it. Let's look at some verses to prove this.

28.) Then they cry unto the Lord in their trouble, and he bringeth them out of their distresses.

29.) He maketh the storm a calm, so that the waves thereof are still.

PSALMS 107:28-29

So you see, GOD Himself calms the storms in our life. That is what the Word of GOD says about it. GOD does not want us having storms in our lives. GOD wants us to have peace. And that goes for storms that are literal storms and storms of a situation that comes up in our lives.

So when you use the Sword of the Spirit, and speak to your mountains and storms, they have to go away.

So when those mountains and storms come up in your lives, be sure to use the Sword of the Spirit on them. Then you will be able to live that abundant victorious life that Jesus wants you to live, and you can enjoy the Bible's full rewards. Because it is indeed The Sword of swords.

Praise the Lord!

# Chapter Seven

---

# Speaking to Fear

S ay to them that are of a fearful heart, Be strong, fear not: behold, your God will come with vengeance, even God with a recompence; he will come and save you.

ISAIAH 35:4

My dear Christian friend, we as Christians are not to fear anything, but God. Satan and his unclean army will come against you to put fear in your heart. That is when you have to know what the Word of GOD says about fear. So you can use it as the Sword of the Spirit and speak to that fear and overcome it.

Our opening verse says clearly to, fear not. It also says GOD will come and save you. That is because GOD does not want you living in fear.

When you fear someone, that fear brings a snare into your life. But when you trust in the Lord, you will be safe from fear. GOD does not want anyone to be living in fear. That is why HE tells us over and over in HIS word to fear not. Let's look at a verse that proves fear brings a snare.

The fear of man bringeth a snare: but whoso putteth his trust in the Lord shall be safe.

PROVERBS 29:25

So you see when you fear someone, it brings a snare into your life. That opens you up for Satan to mess with you in all kinds of ways. But, if you put your trust in the Lord, you will be safe from all danger. That is why it is essential that we as Christians must know what the Word of GOD says about fear. So we can use it as the Sword of the Spirit to overcome all fear when it comes into our lives.

The Lord has not given us a Spirit of fear. That is because he does not want us living in fear. Let's look at a verse to prove this.

For God hath not given us the Spirit of fear; but of power, and of love, and of a sound mind.

2nd TIMOTHY 1:7

So you see, GOD has not given us a Spirit of fear, but of power, and of love, and of a sound mind. You cannot have a sound mind if you are living in fear all of the time. GOD knows that, and that is why HE does not want you living in fear. GOD wants you to have a sound mind.

So now that you know for a fact that GOD does not want you to fear. You know what the Word of GOD says about fear. So when fear comes into your life, you can use the Word of GOD as the Sword of the Spirit and speak to that fear. The confrontation should go something like this.

"Spirit of fear, GOD has not given me a Spirit of fear. The Word of GOD tells me to fear not. So Spirit of fear, I speak to you and I cast you out of my life forever. I will not fear, In Jesus' name."

My dear Christian friend, when you speak to fear like this, you are using the Word of GOD as the Sword of the Spirit and that fear has to leave you for good, no matter what it is that you are fearing.

King David gave us a good example of how to use the Sword of the Spirit against fear. Let's look at a passage to prove this.

1.) The Lord is my light and my Salvation; whom shall I fear? the Lord is the strength of my life; of whom shall I be afraid?

2.) When the wicked, even mine enemies and my foes, came upon me to eat up my flesh, they stumbled and fell.

3.) Though an host should encamp against me, my heart shall not fear: though war should rise against me, in this will I be confident.

PSALMS 27:1-3

King David knew what the Word of GOD said about fear. He said the Lord was his light and his Salvation whom was he to fear. Then he said, "Though an host should encamp against me, my heart shall not fear:." So you see, King David knew that the Word of GOD said to fear not. He knew that GOD was his light and his Salvation. So he said no matter what, his heart shall not fear.

We as Christians are to fear no evil. Nowhere does the Word of GOD say to fear evil. King David gives us another example of how to speak to evil. Let's look at that passage.

yea, though I walk through the valley of the shadow of death, I will fear no evil: for thou art with me; thy rod and thy staff they comfort me.

PSALMS 23:4

So you see, according to this verse, we as Christians are to fear no evil. GOD is always with us, so we have no reason to fear anything. King David knew that the Word of GOD said to fear not and that GOD was always with him. King David knew that the Word of GOD said to be strong and of good courage and not to fear. King David knew that the Lord would not forsake him. So he used the Word of GOD as the Sword of the Spirit and spoke to fear. Let's look at this verse.

Be strong and of a good courage, fear not, nor be afraid of them: for the Lord thy God, he it is that doth go with thee; he will not fail thee, nor forsake thee.

DEUTERONOMY 31:6

So you see, the Word of GOD says not to fear, for GOD will not fail you or forsake you. So when fear comes up in your life, be sure to use the Word of GOD as the Sword of the Spirit and say I will fear no evil.

You already know that we as Christians, are to have peace in Christ. But you cannot have peace if you are living in fear. You are to have peace in your life, because peace is the fruit of the Spirit. But you cannot enjoy the fruit of the Spirit if you are living in fear.

So you must know for a fact that it is not GOD'S Will for you to live in fear. You must know what the Word of GOD says about fear. So you can use it as the Sword of the Spirit to overcome all fear.

Love is fruit of the Spirit also. But, you cannot walk in love like the Word of GOD says to do if you have fear in your life. The Word of GOD tells us to walk in love. Let's look at a verse to prove this.

And walk in love, as Christ also hath loved us, and hath given himself for us an offering and a sacrifice to God for a sweetsmelling savour.

EPHESIANS 5:2

So you see, the Word of GOD tells us to walk in love. That means that you can do it. But not if you have fear in your life. It is GOD'S Will for us to walk in love, and love everyone just as HE loves us. It is not GOD'S Will for us to live in fear.

The Lord will deliver you from all your fears. All you have to do to live fear free is use the Word of GOD as the Sword of the Spirit and speak to your fears and they have to go. Let's look at another verse to prove that GOD will deliver you from all your fears.

I sought the Lord, and he heard me, and delivered me from all my fears.

PSALMS 34:4

So you see, GOD wants to deliver you from all your fears. If you are walking in love in Christ, the fear has to go also. Let's look at a verse to prove this.

There is no fear in love; but perfect love casteth out fear: because fear hath torment. He that feareth is not made perfect in love.

1st JOHN 4:18

So you see, love will cast out the fear. So you can use Scriptures from the Word of GOD on love as the Sword of the Spirit to overcome fear. GOD does not want anyone to be living in fear. That is why HE has made a way for us to live a fear free life. Now you know what the Word of GOD says about fear. It is not GOD'S Will for you.

My friend the best way to defeat fear so you can walk in love is to meet fear with Courage. Let's look at a verse to prove this.

Have not I commanded thee? Be strong and of a good courage; Be not afraid, neither be thou dismayed: for the Lord thy God is with thee whithersoever thou goest.

JOSHUA 1:9

So we can see here that GOD commands us to be of good Courage and to fear not. GOD does not want anyone to live in fear, so HE gave us a way to defeat fear. We are to speak words of Courage from the Word of GOD to our fears, and then we will have victory over that fear.

So when fear comes up in your life, use the Word of GOD as the Sword of the Spirit and overcome that fear. Then you will be able to enjoy the fruit of the Spirit and walk in love.

Then you will be able to live that abundant victorious life that Jesus wants you to live, and you can enjoy the Bible's full rewards. Because it is indeed The Sword of swords.

Hallelujah!

# Chapter Eight

# Speaking to Sin

A fterward Jesus findeth him in the temple, and said unto him, Behold, thou art made whole: sin no more, lest a worse thing come unto thee.

JOHN 5:14

My dear Christian friend, in this verse, Jesus told the man that he had been made whole and to sin no more unless something worse happens to him.

You see, when we sin GOD says to us to sin no more once HE forgives us. When we sin, we step out of Christ and open ourselves up for Satan and his unclean army to bring all kinds of stuff against us.

Satan knows that when we sin, we are stepping out of Christ and that it opens us up for him to steal, kill, and destroy our lives. That is why Satan will do everything in his power to get us to sin.

Satan will use the Word of GOD and turn it around to try to get us to sin. That is why we must know what the Word of GOD says about sin, so we can use it as the Sword of the Spirit and speak to that sin.

GOD has made a way for us to be free from sin. Once we are forgiven of sin and we have our being in Christ, we are free from sin. Let's look at a verse to prove this.

Being then made free from sin, ye became the servants of righteousness.

ROMANS 6:18

So you see, when we are forgiven for sin, we are made free from sin in Christ. So when Satan tries to get you to sin, you can use the Word of GOD as the Sword of the Spirit and say to that sin, "I have been made free from sin, and I will not commit sin anymore in Jesus' name."

The Word of GOD says that whoever commits sin is of the devil. So when Satan tries to get you to sin, you must know what the Word of GOD says about sin so you can use it as the Sword of the Spirit and speak to that sin. Let's look at a verse to prove that whoever commits sin is of the devil.

He that committeth sin is of the devil: for the devil sinneth from the beginning. For this purpose the son of God was manifested, that he might destroy the works of the devil.

1st JOHN 3:8

So you see, the Word of GOD says clearly that whoever sins is of the devil. I know that you do not want to be of the devil at all. So this is why we must know what the Word of GOD says about sin, so we can use it as the Sword of the Spirit and speak to that sin and overcome it.

Nobody should want to sin now that they know it is of the devil. If you sin and you're of the devil, there is no telling what might happen to you.

The devil is out to steal, kill, and destroy your life. Jesus knows that whoever sins is of the devil. That is why HE said sin no more unless a worse thing happen to you. That is because Jesus knows that sin is of the devil, and the devil is only out to steal, kill, and destroy every area of your life.

Jesus wants us to have an abundant victorious life free from sin and Satan's tricks. Let's look at a verse to prove this.

The thief cometh not, but for to steal, and to kill, and to destroy: I am come that they might have life, and that they might have it more abundantly.

JOHN 10:10

So you see, Jesus does not want us to be of the devil and sin. Jesus wants us to have the victory over sin and the devil, and have an abundant victorious life in every area of our lives. So that is why we must have the Word of GOD in us, and know what it says about sin. So we can use it as the Sword of the Spirit and speak to sin.

No I am not saying that we will not sin, because we might. The Word of GOD says that if we say we have not sinned, we make HIM a liar and HIS word is not in us. Let's look at a verse to prove this.

If we say that we have not sinned, we make him a liar, and his word is not in us.

1st JOHN 1:10

So you see, it says the Word of GOD is not in us if we say we have not sinned. The main thing here is to make sure we know what the Word of GOD says about sin, and to have the Word of GOD in us so we will not sin. If we know what the Word of GOD says about sin, and we have the Word of GOD in us, then we can use the Word of GOD as the Sword of the Spirit and speak to sin and overcome it. Remember now, whoever commits sin is of the devil. So you want the Word of GOD in you so you will not sin.

You see, there is no sin in Christ. So when we sin, we step out of Christ and open ourselves up for all kinds of stuff. Let's look at a verse proving that there is no sin in Christ.

And ye know that he was manifested to take away our sins; and in him is no sin.

1st JOHN 3:5

So you see, Christ came to take away our sins. There is no sin in HIM. So when we sin, we step out of Christ and open ourselves up for anything to happen to us. That is why we must know what the Word of GOD says about sin. So we can use it as the Sword of the Spirit and speak to sin and overcome it.

The Word of GOD was written so we would not sin. Let's look at a verse to prove this.

My little Children, these things write I unto you, that ye sin not. And if any man sin, we have an advocate with the Father, Jesus Christ the righteous:

1st JOHN 2:1

So you see, it says these things I write to you that you sin not. The Word of GOD was written so that we would not sin. That is why we must know what the Word of GOD says about sin, so we can use it as the Sword of the Spirit and speak to sin and overcome sin. It says that the Word of GOD was written so we would not sin.

If we do sin and step out of Christ, it is very important that as soon as the Holy Spirit convicts us of that sin, that we ask GOD to forgive us for that sin and get back in Christ before Satan has time to do us harm.

GOD will forgive us for our sins if we confess them to HIM and ask HIM to forgive us for that sin. Let's look at a verse to prove this.

If we confess our sins, he is faithful and just to forgive us our sins, and to cleanse us from all unrighteousness.

1st JOHN 1:9

So you see, if we do sin and step out of Christ, GOD will forgive us for that sin so we can get back in Christ before Satan can harm us.

Now you know what the Word of GOD says about sin. So when Satan tries to get you to sin, you can use the Word of GOD as the Sword of the Spirit and speak to sin.

Then you will be able to live that abundant victorious life that Jesus wants you to live, and you can enjoy the Bible's full rewards. Because it is indeed The Sword of swords.

Glory to GOD!

# Chapter Nine

# Speaking to Unclean Spirits

A nd he called unto him the twelve, and began to send them forth
by two and two; and gave them power over unclean spirits;
MARK 6:7

Dear Powerful People of GOD, according to this verse, Jesus gave
HIS disciples power over unclean, (evil) spirits.

Jesus has given you and me this same great power.

You may not encounter unclean Spirits everywhere you go. But,
then again there is always a chance that you may run into one or more
on any given day.

Everything that occurs in your life may not be the result of unclean
Spirits trying to attack you. So do not look for demonic activity in each
and every situation you encounter.

However, the Word of GOD speaks clearly of a Spiritual war between GOD, GOD'S angels, GOD'S people, and our guardian angels
against evil, unclean Spirits.

Just as Satan, (The thief) mentioned in JOHN 10:10, is out to steal, kill, and destroy the Christian's life, so is the rest of his unclean army.

These unclean Spirits are out to steal, kill, and destroy us in every area of our lives. They war against our angels to hinder our prayers from being manifested in our lives.

They also war against you and I to influence us to doubt what GOD'S Word says we can be, do, and have here on earth, and to hinder that.

The Word of GOD, also described as the Sword of the Spirit, is our chief weapon that GOD has given us to overpower these demonic forces.

The "Sword" can be described as the following:

"SWORD"

"S"piritual

"W"ords

"O"verpowering

"R"eal

"D"emons

GOD'S Word is Spirit that is why it is referred to as the Sword of the Spirit. (JOHN 6:63; EPHESIANS 6:17)

When we speak GOD'S Word as the Sword of the Spirit, something happens in the Spiritual realm, GOD'S angels, and our angels go to war to give these words substance, and to manifest that substance, (whatever we desire) here in the natural realm.

Let's look at a verse to prove this.

Bless the LORD, ye his angels, that excel in strength, that do his commandments, hearkening unto the voice of his word.

PSALMS 103:20

So as we see here, GOD'S angels do HIS commandments, (HIS Word), and they hearken unto the voice of HIS Word.

When you and I speak GOD'S Word as the Sword of the Spirit, mighty angels hearken, (pay attention) to our voice, the voice of HIS Word. Then they set out in the Spiritual realm to do HIS commandments, (HIS Word) that we speak into our situations, and to those unclean Spirits that we are in war against.

Our angels are in combat, continuously defending us, and fighting unclean Spirits that are trying to hinder GOD'S Word from being manifested in our lives by our angels.

All of those unclean Spirits must eventually bow the knee when we use GOD'S Word as the Sword of the Spirit, and especially when we speak it in the name of Jesus.

Always remember that the battle is not flesh and blood. Our battle is not against people, but unclean Spirits working through people.

Let's look at a verse to prove this.

For we wrestle not against flesh and blood, but against Principalities, against powers, against the rulers of darkness of this world, against Spiritual wickedness in high places.

EPHESIANS 6:12

So you see, according to this verse, we are not battling flesh and blood, (People).

So never use the Sword on people. It is essential that you always recognize the Spirit behind the people. So never speak to the person, but the Spirit that is influencing the person.

Let's look at a passage to prove this.

22.) Then Peter took him, and began to rebuke him, saying, Be it far from thee, Lord: this shall not be unto thee.

23.) But he turned, and said unto Peter. Get thee behind me, Satan: thou art an offence unto me: for thou savourest not the things that be of God, but those that be of men.

MATTHEW 16:22-23

Now this passage appears that Jesus was speaking to Peter. But notice whose name Jesus called, (Satan). So actually Jesus was speaking to the Spirit that was working through Peter, which was Satan. Jesus told Satan that he was an offence to HIM, because Satan was not of the things of GOD.

So it is with Satan and his unclean army today. They do everything they can to prevent us from receiving the things that are of GOD in our lives. GOD is out to bless us in every area of our lives. But, Satan and his unclean army are out to steal, kill, and destroy those blessings. You can see that GOD wants to bless us in (PSALMS 115:12-14), and you can see that the thief, (Satan) is out to steal, kill, and destroy us, and our blessings. (JOHN 10:10)

Never get angry at people when an unclean Spirit is working through them to get to you. One thing that will help you in this area is, if you will acknowledge that they are not coming against you, but Christ in you. And Glory to GOD the Word of GOD says, greater is HE that is in us, than he that is in the world. (1st JOHN 4:4)

Jesus told us that if the world hates us, we should recognize that it hated HIM first. Let's look at a verse to prove this.

If the world hate you, ye know that it hated me before it hated you. JOHN 15:18

So you see, those unclean Spirits that are in the world hate Jesus. So always acknowledge that when an unclean Spirit works through someone to come against you. Actually, the unclean Spirit hates the Christ in you, and wants to come against Christ in you.

Jesus even went on to say that HE told us those things so we would not be offended. (JOHN 16:1)

So never be offended when you encounter an unclean Spirit working through someone to attack Christ in you.

Even though the unclean Spirits are attacking the Christ in you, ultimately it affects you and me in many ways. Here are some ways we may be affected by them.

1.) They will try to distract us from serving GOD.

2.) They will try to disrupt our relationship with GOD.

3.) They will try to steal our love, joy, peace, and all the fruits of the Spirit mentioned in GALATIANS 5:22-23.

4.) They will try to steal our testimony.

5.) They will try to slander us to keep us from becoming effective witnesses for Jesus Christ.

6.) They will tempt us to sin.

7.) They will try to steal our blessings and prevent us from being, doing, and having all of the things GOD'S Word says we can be, do, and have.

So ultimately these attacks of these unclean Spirits against the Christ in us, will have an effect on us.

That is why we need the Sword of the Spirit. GOD told us in HIS word to take it. HE is basically saying we are going to need it, to take it and use it.

Let's look at a verse to prove this.

And "take" the helmet of Salvation, and the Sword of the Spirit, which is the word of God.

EPHESIANS 6:17

So what GOD is telling us here is, to "take" the Sword of the Spirit. HE is saying take it, because you are going to need it.

Remember that we have angels on standby just waiting for us to use GOD'S Word as the Sword of the Spirit. If you never use GOD'S Word as the Sword of the Spirit, your angels will not have anything on your behalf to destroy the work of those unclean Spirits, or to manifest your blessings.

Remember that GOD'S Word, (The Sword of the Spirit) is what moves our angels. (PSALMS 103:20) So if you have a situation that looks like there is no hope of defeating, or that your blessing may never come. Maybe all you need is one verse from GOD'S Word to speak as the Sword of the Spirit to help your angels win you the victory, and to manifest your blessings.

In the book of DANIEL, we see that Daniel prayed GOD'S Word, and that as he did, it moved mighty angels on his behalf. Let's look at verses to prove this.

3.) And I set my face unto the Lord God, to seek by prayer and supplications, with fasting, and sackcloth, and ashes:

4.) And I prayed unto the LORD my God, and made my confession, and said, O Lord, the great and dreadful God, keeping the covenant and mercy to them that love him, and to them that keep his Commandments.

DANIEL 9:3-4

So as we see here, Daniel spoke and prayed GOD'S Word from DEUTERONOMY 7:9, and the angels moved on his behalf, because of the Word of GOD that he spoke and prayed.

Let's look at a passage to prove this.

"The angel appeared and said this to Daniel."

12.) Then said he unto me, Fear not, Daniel: for from the first day that thou didst set thine heart to understand, and to Chasten thyself before thy God, thy words were heard, and I am come for thy words.

DANIEL 10:12

So you see, the angel told Daniel that his words were heard the first day, and that he, (the angel) came for his words.

Daniel's words were actually GOD'S Word, (The Sword of the Spirit) that moved those angels and they came because of his words, which were actually GOD'S words.

The angels went to war as soon as Daniel spoke, or prayed GOD'S Word. But, unclean Spirits also went to war to prevent Daniel's angels from appearing to Daniel with the answer.

Let's look at what else the angel said to Daniel.

13.) But the Prince of the Kingdom of Persia withstood me one and twenty days: but, lo, Michael, one of the Chief Princes, came to help me; and I remained there with the Kings of Persia.

DANIEL 10:13

So we see here that unclean Spirits, the Prince of the Kingdom of Persia withstood, fought against Daniel's angel to prevent Daniel's words from coming to pass. But, Praise the Lord, GOD sent Daniel's angel some help, Michael the Archangel, and together they won the battle.

It may sometimes appear that these unclean Spirits have you outnumbered, or that they are working through many people to attack you. But, be of Good Cheer, because we, as GOD'S people have more angels on our side that are far more powerful than the unclean Spirits that we encounter.

One thing that will help you in this area is, if you will look beyond what the unclean Spirits are doing, and see what your angels are doing.

Elisha and his Servant found themselves in a situation that looked like they were outnumbered and the Servant couldn't see anything, but the enemy who appeared to have them outnumbered. Then Elisha asked GOD to open the Servant's eyes so that he could see, and GOD showed the Servant that he and Elisha had more angels protecting them than the enemy had on their side.

Let's look at a passage to prove this.

14.) Therefore sent he thither horses, and Chariots, and a great host: and they came by night, and compassed the city about.

15.) And when the Servant of the man of God was risen early, and gone forth, behold, an host compassed the city both with horses and Chariots. And his Servant said unto him, Alas my Master! how shall we do?

16.) And he answered, Fear not: for they that be with us are more than they that be with them.

17.) And Elisha prayed, and said, LORD, I pray thee, open his eyes, that he may see. And the LORD opened the eyes of the young man; and he saw: and, behold, the mountain was full of horses and Chariots of fire about Elisha.

2nd KINGS 6:14-17

In this passage, the situation looked hopeless to the Servant of the man of GOD. It appeared that they were defeated. But, when the man of GOD prayed, and GOD opened the Servant's eyes, he could then see that he and Elisha had far more angels for them than there was against them.

Look at what happened to the people that the unclean Spirits were working through when the man of GOD spoke, or prayed GOD'S Word against them.

18.) And when they came down to him, Elisha prayed unto the LORD, and said, smite this people, I pray thee, with blindness. And he smote them with blindness according to the word of Elisha.

2nd KINGS 6:18

When Elisha prayed, this verse says that the LORD smote these people with blindness, according to the word of Elisha. So we see that something happened as a result of the words that Elisha prayed or spoke.

Take note that in this verse, when Elisha asked the Lord to strike the people with blindness, that actually Elisha was praying or speaking GOD'S Word from GENESIS 19:1-11, where a man of GOD'S angels struck the enemy with blindness. So actually Elisha was praying or speaking the Word of GOD, which is the Sword of the Spirit.

So when the unclean Spirits had Elisha's Servant blinded to what their angels were doing, Elisha turned it around and blinded the enemies with the same blindness. Now that is what I call fighting fire with fire. Hallelujah!

So when you feel that you have unclean Spirits working through everyone you encounter, and it seems you are outnumbered, take heart, because one verse from GOD'S Word can turn the entire situation around in your favor.

So now we know that the battle is not flesh and blood, it is not against people, but unclean Spirits working through people, and we are never outnumbered.

Another thing that will help you when you look beyond the person and see the Spirit behind the person, which is really bad, is if you will look for the good in the person. If you acknowledge that the person is good, and you esteem the person higher than yourself, you will overcome the evil unclean Spirit that is working through the person.

Let's look at a few verses to prove this.

3.) Let nothing be done through strife or vain glory; but in lowliness of mind let each esteem other better than themselves.

4.) Look not every man on his own things, but every man also on the things of others.

PHILIPPIANS 2:3-4

So as you see, according to these verses, we are to esteem others better than ourselves, and not look at our own things, (our situations), but look every man on the things of others. So if we look at the people that the unclean Spirits are working through, and esteem them better than ourselves, we will see the good in the people, yet see the bad in the unclean Spirits working through the people.

The Word of GOD also tells us not to be overcome by evil, but to overcome evil with good. So we are not to be overcome by the evil, unclean Spirit that works through the people, but we are to look beyond it to the good in the people and overcome the evil with good.

Let's look at a verse to prove this.

21.) Be not overcome of evil, but overcome evil with good.

ROMANS 12:21

So always look for the good in the person, but acknowledge the evil coming from the unclean Spirit that is working through them.

By doing this, you will always come out victorious, and overcome the evil with good. We also know that the Word of GOD is good. So, when you speak the good Word of GOD to the evil, unclean Spirits it is then that you will have the victory, and without a doubt, overcome evil with good, the good Word of GOD. The good Sword of the Spirit will bring us victory over all unclean Spirits when we speak the Word of GOD as the Sword of the Spirit. The Word of GOD refers to itself as the good Word of GOD in HEBREWS 6:5.

The Word of GOD, when used as the Sword of the Spirit, is quick and powerful, and sharper than any two edged sword.

Let's look at a verse to prove this.

For the word of God is quick, and powerful, and sharper than any two edged sword, piercing even to the dividing asunder of soul and Spirit, and of the joints and marrow, and is a discerner of the thoughts and intents of the heart.

HEBREWS 4:12

My dear Christian friend, the Word of GOD is without a doubt the most powerful thing on this earth. GOD has given us this mighty weapon to use against unclean, evil Spirits and it will do the job. The Sword of the Spirit when spoken from our mouth, will send those unclean Spirits running in every direction. That is because it is The

Word of GOD, and they won't know if it is us or GOD Himself speaking to them.

So now you know what the Word of GOD says about us having power over unclean Spirits.

You also know that you must use the Word of GOD as the Sword of the Spirit to overpower those unclean Spirits so that you will have victory in your life.

So when unclean Spirits arise in your life, take the Word of GOD and use it as the Sword of the Spirit and overcome those unclean Spirits. Then you will be able to enjoy the abundant life that Jesus has provided for you. (JOHN 10:10)

Then you will be able to live that abundant victorious life that Jesus wants you to live, and you can enjoy the Bible's full rewards. Because it is indeed The Sword of swords.

Hallelujah!

# Chapter Ten

---

# The Final
# Authority

A nd whatsoever ye do in word or deed, do all in the name of the
Lord Jesus, giving thanks to God and the Father by him.
COLOSSIANS 3:17

My dear Christian friend, the final authority when you use the
Word of GOD as the Sword of the Spirit, is the name of Jesus. The
name of Jesus is what gives the Sword of the Spirit power to accomplish whatever you use it for.

According to our opening verse, whatever we do, in word or deed,
we are to do it in the name of Jesus. That means when you use the
Word of GOD as the Sword of the Spirit and speak it to a situation,
you must use the name of Jesus or it won't have any power.

When you pray you must use the name of Jesus. It is the same way
when you are using the Word of GOD as the Sword of the Spirit. You
must do it in the name of Jesus. According to our opening verse, we
are to do all in the name of Jesus. This verse says whatever you do in
word, do in the name of Jesus. That means if you are speaking, do it in

the name of Jesus. The name of Jesus is the final authority and power when you are using the Word of GOD as the Sword of the Spirit.

My dear Christian friend, we are to do everything we do in the name of Jesus. When you cast out a devil or an unclean Spirit, you are to do it in the name of Jesus. When you bring forth a message in tongues, you are to do it in the name of Jesus. When you lay hands on the sick to heal them, you are to do it in the name of Jesus. We are to do all in the name of Jesus. Let's look at a passage to prove this.

15.) And he said unto them, Go ye into all the world, and Preach the gospel to every Creature.

16.) He that believeth and is baptized shall be saved; but he that believeth not shall be damned.

17.) And these signs shall follow them that believe; In my name shall they cast out devils; they shall speak with new tongues;

18.) They shall take up serpents; and if they drink any deadly thing, it shall not hurt them; they shall lay hands on the sick, and they shall recover.

MARK 16:15-18

So you see, this passage says we can do all of those things in the name of Jesus. We can cast out devils or unclean Spirits in the name of Jesus. We can speak in tongues in the name of Jesus. We can lay hands on the sick for their healing in the name of Jesus. We can do everything mentioned in this passage, but we must do it in the name of Jesus.

That is because the name of Jesus is the final authority. When you do anything in this passage, you can use the Word of GOD as the Sword of the Spirit to do it. You can say, devil or unclean Spirit, the Word of GOD says I can cast you out, So I cast you out In Jesus' Name. You can say to the sick, the Word of GOD says I can lay hands on the sick and they will recover, So sickness, I command you to leave this person, and I speak healing into them in Jesus' Name.

When you use the Word of GOD like this, you have just used it as the Sword of the Spirit. But remember, you must do it in the name of Jesus. Because the name of Jesus is the final authority. The name of Jesus is indeed what gives the Sword of the Spirit the power to accomplish whatever you are using it for.

You see, GOD Himself is the one who told Jesus what to speak. Let's look at a verse to prove this.

For I have not spoken of myself; but the Father which sent me, he gave me a Commandment, what I should say, and what I should speak.

JOHN 12:49

So you see, GOD was the one who told Jesus what to say and speak. So when Jesus gave us his name to use, GOD was the one who told HIM to do it. The name of Jesus is what gives the Sword of the Spirit the power to accomplish anything you use it for. That is because Jesus has been given all power. Let's look at a verse to prove this.

And Jesus came and spake unto them, saying, All Power is given unto me in heaven and in earth.

MATTHEW 28:18

So if Jesus said HE has been given all power and GOD was the one telling HIM what to speak, then GOD gave Jesus all power. That is why the name of Jesus is the final authority and what gives the Word of GOD power when we use it as the Sword of the Spirit.

GOD Himself is the one who told us whatever we do, to do in the name of Jesus. GOD Himself gave us the Sword of the Spirit to use in any situation we may face in this life.

Let's look at an example of where an unclean Spirit was cast out in Jesus' name.

16.) And it came to pass, as we went to prayer, a certain damsel possessed with a Spirit of divination met us, which brought her masters much gain by soothsaying:

17.) The same followed Paul and us, and cried, saying, These men are the Servants of the most high God, which shew unto us the way of Salvation.

18.) And this did she many days. But Paul, being grieved, turned and said to the Spirit, I command thee in the name of Jesus Christ to come out of her. And he came out the same hour.

ACTS 16:16-18

So you see, Paul gave us a good example of how to cast out an unclean Spirit in Jesus' name. Paul said I command thee in Jesus' name to come out of her. The unclean Spirit came out, because Paul used the name of Jesus.

This is not just an example of what happens when you cast out an unclean Spirit in Jesus' name.

This is a good example of the mighty power of Jesus' name.

Like I said earlier in this book, the Sword of the Spirit is the most powerful thing on this earth.

But when you use the Word of GOD as the Sword of the Spirit, you must do it in the name of Jesus.

The name of Jesus is the final authority, and what gives the Sword of the Spirit its power.

When you use the Word of GOD as the Sword of the Spirit in Jesus' name, it will accomplish anything that you are using it for. If you use the Word of GOD as the Sword of the Spirit concerning anything I have mentioned to you in this book, it will accomplish whatever you need.

The Sword of the Spirit is the only thing we as Christians need to face and overcome any situation we may face in our lives. When you use the Word of GOD as the Sword of the Spirit in Jesus' name, you are assured to have the victory in that situation.

So when anything this world has to offer comes into your life, grab the Sword of the Spirit and get the victory in that situation.

Then you will be able to live that abundant, victorious life that Jesus wants you to live, and you can enjoy the Bible's full rewards. Because it is indeed The Sword of Swords.

Hallelujah!

# Power Prayer

For Salvation and to be baptized in the Holy Spirit.

Father GOD, I come to you as humbly as I know how. Lord, your word says in 1st JOHN 1:9, "If we confess our sins, he is faithful and just to forgive us our sins, and to cleanse us from all unrighteousness." So I confess to you that I have sinned in many ways. I now repent and turn away from my sins and I ask you to forgive me and cleanse me from all of my unrighteousness, in the name of Jesus.

Father, your word also says in ROMANS 10:9-10, "That if thou shalt confess with thy mouth the Lord Jesus, and shalt believe in thine heart that God raised him from the dead, thou shalt be saved. For with the heart man believeth unto righteousness; and with the mouth confession is made unto Salvation."

So I confess with my mouth that I believe Jesus died on the Cross so I can be saved and I believe with all my heart, that GOD raised HIM from the dead and I ask you to come into my life and save me. I now accept Jesus as my Lord and Savior and I believe with all my heart that your word is true, and that I am saved by grace!

Father, your word also says in the Book of LUKE 11:13, "If ye then being evil, know how to give good gifts unto your children: how much more shall your heavenly Father give the Holy Spirit to them that ask him?"

So Father, I ask you to give me the gift of the Holy Spirit. I ask you to fill me till my cup runs over and allow me to successfully function in the gifts of the Spirit that are mentioned in your word. So that I will become an effective witness for Jesus and a blessing to others for the rest of my life. In Jesus' name I pray, Amen.

If you prayed this prayer, you can believe without a doubt that you are saved. The Bible says, "you shall be saved." That is a promise, and it is also a promise that GOD will fill you with the Holy Spirit if you ask HIM.

So, now, you need to join a good church and sincerely turn away from your old sinful life and walk in and enjoy the new Spirit-filled life that GOD has given you. The old you should start fading into the past, and the new you will start shining brightly as you seek to serve GOD in all that you do.

# About the author

Thomas Couch has a GED, and some college credits (no degree) with MERCER, and BREWTON PARKER Universities. He was an Honor Roll student while he attended college.

The name of his ministry is "REVIVE-ALL Ministries. This Ministry is an outreach of "Souls Harbor Word of Faith Church" in Canton, Georgia. Where he was ordained and licensed to minister as a Preacher of the Gospel. He has a Certificate for "Caring for People God's Way" with Light University, that is approved by the American Association of Christian Counselors Board.

He is currently a member of the Colorful Crow Writers Community, and engaged in a writing ministry.

GOD gave Thomas this material to write in efforts to minister to GOD'S people, to reach the lost, and to abundantly bless all who will enjoy its contents.

He says it is proof that with GOD you can do all things through Christ who strengthens you. (PHILIPPIANS 4:13)

He prays it will be a blessing to everyone it reaches.

www.ingramcontent.com/pod-product-compliance
Lightning Source LLC
Chambersburg PA
CBHW071217120626
46546CB00006B/2598